THE ?

"Sandra's book is a valuable reminder of why PR has always had the power to do so much more than just communicate. She inspires marketers and PR practitioners to think differently about how to connect with our stakeholders."

ADAM FRIEDMAN

Vice President and General Manager

"Sandra's combined skills as a seasoned practitioner and inspiring professor make her one of the most valuable voices in the industry today. In The Smart PR Book, she creates an essential, interactive experience for learners, leaders and strategic doers."

NANCY R. TAG

Professor and Founding Director, Branding + Integrated Communications (BIC) graduate program at The City College of New York

"Sandra captures in her book that public relations and storytelling is about empathy and humanity, and the skills that make us great practitioners are the ones that help us authentically connect with clients and stakeholders. She shows how PR professionals can help create trust, collaboration and, ultimately, be a lynchpin for progress in the world! This book is a must-read for anyone entering or already working in the field."

KATHY BLOOMGARDEN

CEO, Ruder Finn

"*The Smart PR Book is required reading for anyone considering a career in public relations, as well as professionals looking to finetune and upgrade their skillset.*"

STEVE CODY

Founder and CEO, Peppercomm, co-author, *The ROI of LOL: How Laughter Breaks Down Walls, Drives Compelling Storytelling and Creates a Healthy Workplace*

"*Sandra gives readers a window inside her mind – clear thinking, relentless creativity and an energetic 'yes' mindset. Her dedication to the art and craft of PR for the last 30+ years is inspiring, and* The Smart PR Book *contains countless enduring lessons for communicators, businesspeople and the simply curious among us.*"

SOPHIE JACOB

Head of Internal Communications, Blue Owl Capital

"*The Smart PR Book is a timely, insightful guide that brings the evolving world of public relations to life. Sandra is a senior PR advisor for whom I have enormous respect. Her interactive, hands-on approach and focus on digital, tech and other aspects that work together for communications and reputation management make this a valuable practical book for both newcomers and experienced PR professionals alike.*"

PAVAN R. CHAWLA

Founder-Editor, Mediabrief.com, and host of the award-winning MVP – The Masters Voice Podcast

"*The best PR professionals are life-long learners. Whether you have years of experience already or are a student looking to break into this career, Sandra Stahl's* The Smart PR Book *is a resource youll find yourself returning to time and again.*"

PETER WALPOLE

Senior Manager, Corporate Digital, Golin, Lecturer, City College of New York

FOR OTHER TITLES IN THE SERIES ...

CONCISE ADVICE LAB

SMALL BOOKS: BIG IDEAS

CLEVER CONTENT, DYNAMIC IDEAS, PRACTICAL
SOLUTIONS AND ENGAGING VISUALS –
A CATALYST TO INSPIRE NEW WAYS OF THINKING
AND PROBLEM-SOLVING IN A COMPLEX WORLD

www.lidpublishing.com/product-category/concise-advice-series

Published by
LID Publishing
An imprint of LID Business Media Ltd.
LABS House, 15–19 Bloomsbury Way,
London, WC1A 2TH, UK

info@lidpublishing.com
www.lidpublishing.com

A member of:

businesspublishersroundtable.com

Printed and bound in Great Britain by Halstan Ltd.

ISBN: 978-1-915951-67-0
ISBN: 978-1-915951-68-7 (ebook)

Cover and page design: Caroline Li

THE SMART PR BOOK

A PRACTICAL GUIDE TO
THE ART & CRAFT OF PUBLIC RELATIONS

SANDRA STAHL

MADRID | MEXICO CITY | LONDON
BUENOS AIRES | BOGOTA | SHANGHAI

For my parents, Rae and Irwin Stahl

CONTENTS

PROLOGUE   viii

1. PR IS NOT LIMITED   1
2. HOW PR BEGAN   9
3. CORE TENETS   14
4. PR FUNDAMENTALS   21
5. THINK ATTRACTION, NOT PROMOTION   35
6. THINK MEANINGFUL, NOT JUST 'SNACKABLE,' CONTENT   42
7. CREATIVITY   47
8. LISTEN   56
9. WORDS ARE OUR CURRENCY   66
10. CALL TO ACTION   78
11. TECHNOLOGY REVOLUTION   85
12. THE HARD WORK OF BUILDING A GOOD CORPORATE REPUTATION   90
13. THE MEDIA   96
14. PERFECTION IS OVERRATED   100
15. YOUR JOURNEY TO SMART PR   106

RESOURCES AND FURTHER READING   108

ACKNOWLEDGMENTS   114
ABOUT THE AUTHOR   116

PROLOGUE

The other day, I was speaking with a couple of friends after yoga about our children. I shared that my daughter, Sophie, just changed jobs and now she was the head of internal communications at a leading alternative asset manager. My friends – both accomplished lawyers – said, "That's great. Congratulations! So tell me, what does she do?" After I explained a bit, they said, "Oh right, that makes sense. Sophie was always such a good writer."

The exchange reminded me of when I told my parents that I was going to focus on a career in PR. And when I got a job at an agency, they would proudly tell people where I was working along with something like, "You know, she always liked to talk." My father never stopped saying I was "a people person."

Later, when I'd tell them about the medicine I helped launch, or the crisis team I was on, or how I was using communications to add clarity to a complicated issue that was negatively impacting my client's business, my mother would say in a disappointed voice that I was making people think they were sick. But I'd persist. I'd explain how my work connected people from inside and outside a company, provided valuable information people needed to know, addressed health care access and affordability, and built (or rebuilt) a company's reputation among stakeholders and in communities.

At the end of these conversations, Mom would inevitably nod and say, "OK, I understand. But which part was PR?"

My parents and friends are not alone in misunderstanding PR or even the broader realm of communications and tend to reduce it to specific skills. What is and is not public relations remains hard to define, even since I first wrote about this topic in *The Art & Craft of PR*. Where PR begins and ends, the point at which it evolves into something else, such as marketing or branding, is still dissected on a practically Talmudic level.

Considering PR a part of communications is certainly one popular point of view, though others say that communications is a subset of PR; that communications is just a tool in a comprehensive PR toolbox we use to connect with stakeholders.

Whichever definition you choose to apply, one thing on which nearly all agree is that it is the holistic definition of PR – not just one part of it or another – that ultimately matters. And that's because PR has a different endgame from other disciplines: The creation of meaningful relationships that contribute to the achievement of larger goals. There are many paths to meaningful relationships. It is this connection, and not the tactics or channels used to get there, that truly defines PR and has earned and secured its place of value in the business world.

THE MYTHS

An ongoing misperception of PR is that practitioners can somehow get a client or a story on the cover of *The Wall Street Journal* or be the top story on CNN. That we wave a wand and a positive article about the company or brand magically appears. Here's another:

PR is 'spin' – that practitioners can somehow make a negative sound like a positive. Finally, here is one I have, stunningly, just encountered: If PR doesn't include writing and issuing press releases, what is it? And why do I need to pay for it? Readers will learn, in this book, about the valuable role of PR – what it is all about and what it is not.

THE ART & CRAFT OF PR

Our ability to articulate a position – what a company or brand stands for, its values and goals – is part of that process. Add to that the reading and understanding of a situation, the insight underpinning the foundation and scale of that relationship and what's needed. This is what I'd call the art of PR.

Mastery of the tools we use to bring that articulation and the relationship to life is the craft. PR professionals must be proficient in the language and mechanics of a wide variety of platforms and channels – from the digital, interactive and social to the traditional, mainstream and community-based, as well as the power of word-of-mouth. We need to be facile and diligent and aware of the benefits and potential pitfalls of all of these, given how many have been used to perpetrate disinformation and misinformation.

What's important to realize about the craft is that many of these same tools and channels are available to other service providers outside of PR. What makes PR a distinct and valued discipline is our ability to *combine* the art and the craft. Equipped with strong skills in both, PR people can well and truly support public affairs, public policy, analyst and investor relations, marketing, brands, corporate reputation, internal comms, change management and business executives throughout an organization. Why? Because we are adept at reading the spoken and behavioral cues of a target audience, building a meaningful and enduring relationship, and articulating the message, culture or philosophy of the organization, brand or company we're representing, skillfully using all the tools at our disposal.

Our skills as relationship builders using strategy, storytelling and influence can take PR in an infinite number of directions. Communicating a point of view persuasively, building a relationship that prompts an action, changing minds, creating preference, building community, managing a crisis – it's all PR.

WHAT YOU'LL FIND IN THIS BOOK

PR is and has always been distinct. Its value is not confined to practitioners' ability to master the latest tools. For example, Artificial Intelligence (AI) technology, while changing the way we do some of our work in PR, is also used in many industries. We don't have a 'swim lane' or a 'silo' that confines our professional capabilities or governs our growth.

Throughout these pages, readers will find a users' manual for developing and nurturing the mindset required for the art of PR, together with the fundamental skills for executing the craft. It is not necessary to embrace and practice all the recommendations you'll find here to achieve success. Instead, I offer you here a portfolio of strategies and insights, as well as exercises – some of which I hope you'll find to be thought provoking and fun – that will inspire PR practitioners of today and tomorrow.

"

If I was down to the last dollar of my marketing budget, I'd spend it on PR.

"

Bill Gates

CHAPTER 1
PR IS NOT LIMITED

Many years ago, Jeremy Jacob, my partner in jacobstahl, our integrated communications agency, worked for View-Master, maker of the classic toy that brought the world to children through special plastic scopes and cardboard circles of color transparencies. His client, Elliot, was about the same age as Jeremy and considered the marketing maverick at his company.

One day, Elliot came to the office to discuss the launch of a new View-Master offering called Kidsongs, a series of upbeat live-action music videos of well-known tunes to get kids aged 1–8 up and moving. Like the product, the marketing communications needed to go beyond the expected. Elliot immediately turned to PR for the solution and, as inspiration, told Jeremy to go back to his "rock and roll roots" to develop a plan that, in today's vernacular, would be described as disruptive.

He expected PR to meet his communications challenge with something new and different that would surprise and delight the target audience. To facilitate that, he asked PR to lead the marketing effort. Why? Because PR is not just one form of communication. The ever-expanding PR toolbox can lend itself to any challenge or opportunity.

Indeed, some of the most celebrated campaigns in recent years have been PR-led. Procter & Gamble's #LikeAGirl campaign for Always, the feminine hygiene brand, started with PR and the insight that women experienced a decline in confidence at puberty, and casual use of the phrase, 'like a girl' (as in, 'walks like a girl' or 'throws like a girl') added insult to injury. The centerpiece of the first campaign was a powerful video, and the effort has grown over the years to include a television ad aired during the Super Bowl.

Empowerment is a strong cornerstone of purpose-driven campaigns. Consider 'Fearless Girl,' commissioned by asset management company State Street Global Advisors. The campaign featured a statue of a determined-looking young lady dropped on Wall Street in the middle of the night. She was positioned facing down the iconic charging bull statue and became a global phenomenon within 24 hours. State Street's purpose was to "ignite a conversation about the importance of gender diversity in corporate leadership." This campaign sparked conversation, opened doors, was covered in the media, and has been talked about and admired for years. The financial services firm continued investing in it, and in 2021 installed a broken glass ceiling around the statue to symbolize the many barriers to advancement women have shattered. I walk by 'Fearless Girl' regularly and it continues to be a source of inspiration.

Jeremy Jacob

PR is also the discipline many turn to for tapping into popular culture and creating shared experiences. Among my favorite examples is when Mountain Dew, the soft drink brand, sponsored a lively party at a senior living community in Florida. Typically a brand that targeted millennials or college students, Mountain Dew brought a spring break-type bash – complete with live music, limbo dancing, cocktails and selfies – to an older audience who, based on the media coverage that followed, loved it.

Of course, as a fellow PR practitioner I recognize the strategies of these campaigns and admire how they've been brought to life. I love how they showcase the thoughtfulness and creativity of our discipline and appreciate the halo they bring to the business I'm in. But mostly, I appreciate these campaigns because they are successful and universally relatable.

There's nothing in PR that limits us strategically or tactically.

Circling back to Elliot and View-Master, the PR solution leaned into the 'classic' nature of the brand and the songs. The final campaign brought these songs, with the nostalgia and warm feelings they evoked, to life at Toy Fair, the premier 'can't miss' event for the toy industry, and for consumers in key markets. The PR led to a multi-million dollar advertising effort featuring Mariette Hartley, a film and television personality beloved for her classic wholesomeness.

PR can lead any communications challenge. It can uncover the insights, create the relationships, spark media coverage and word-of-mouth awareness, and provide the foundation for all kinds of communications answers. There's nothing in PR that limits us strategically or tactically.

TIPS FOR HOW TO BEGIN DEVELOPING A PR CAMPAIGN

START WITH THE END IN MIND: Consider what success looks like – what you'd really like to achieve, how you'd like stakeholders to feel and what you'd like them to do after they experience your messaging and campaign. Then, back into your strategy and ideas.

PLACE YOURSELF IN THE SHOES OF THE STAKEHOLDER AUDIENCE: And then, from that vantage point, let insights derived from that understanding drive strategy and tactics.

<u>LEARN THE BUSINESS OF THE BRAND YOU'RE REPRESENTING</u>: It all starts with a strong sense of business. You need to know the objective of the company or issue you're supporting, how communications fits in, and to what end. You also need to understand every element of the business of the company or organization you're representing, whether it's a corporation, organization or non-profit. You need a grasp of not only communications, but also finance, marketing, employee relations, investor relations, government oversight and policies – really, the entire ecosystem in which you're operating.

<u>GREAT IDEAS CAN COME FROM ANYWHERE</u>: PR practitioners have the imaginative chops to tackle an ever-widening array of challenges and serve as the primary communications catalyst for any brand challenge. Inspiration for great ideas can be found everywhere: daily people-watching, workplace and popular culture, the news, editorial opinion, books – great literature, non-fiction and popular fiction – as well as everyday conversations. This is why I always encourage my teams and students (and myself) to say 'yes' more than 'no' to networking opportunities, cocktail parties and book launches – essentially, anywhere to meet new people, have conversations and absorb new thoughts and ideas. Sometimes these events feel like work. Sometimes they *are* work. Regardless, it is always the case that those who seize opportunities are the ones who succeed.

Embracing the freedoms inherent in our discipline empowers us to restate the value of public relations at a time when many of the issues companies face stem from a failure to engage with the right stakeholders, in the right way, at the right time. They come about through misjudgment or misreading of various stakeholder groups and what's important to them. Returning to the 'relationships' that result from public relations – and what makes strong, trusted ones – will always stand communications, practitioners and the brands and companies we represent in good stead.

"

Some are born great; some achieve greatness; and some hire public relations officers.

"

Daniel J. Boorstin

CHAPTER 2
HOW PR BEGAN

The roots of public relations are instructive and inspiring. I encourage learning about the industry's founders and early work. Let's take a step back now to look at how PR all began.

The origins of public relations can be traced to Ancient Greece, where philosophers such as Plato and Aristotle wrote about the art of rhetoric in persuasion. Later, in the 17th century, communications in the form of books, leaflets and lectures were used to sway public opinion toward abolishing the slave trade.

But it was in the 20th century, with the birth of mass communication, that public relations as a discipline – and the industry we know today – was born. While there is some disagreement over who 'founded' PR, Austrian-American Edward L. Bernays, who died in 1995 at the age of 103, is most recognized as the forefather of modern-day PR. The nephew of Sigmund Freud, he pioneered many techniques for influencing public opinion, which he called "engineering of consent."

My favorite part of Bernays' approach is that he never lost sight of the practical business value of PR. "Public relations, effectively used, helps validate an underlying principle of our society – competition in the marketplace of ideas and things," he wrote in 1971, as reported in his obituary in *The New York Times*.

One of many misunderstandings about PR is the idea that if you want to get a story in a major media outlet, you call in your PR team. Tactically, Bernays went far beyond media relations, or what he termed *press agentry*, though he had great success generating publicity for his clients. Besides 'earned media' – press coverage that is not bought as with advertising – he used endorsements from opinion leaders, celebrities, doctors and other experts as part of his campaigns. That's a technique we might refer to these days as an influencer strategy.

He employed many other PR tools still in use: consistent messaging, public opinion polls, events, word of mouth. One well-known campaign he orchestrated was for Ivory soap. The objective was to make bathing more popular with children. The solution: He surveyed consumers and found that most preferred soap to be simple – plain, white, non-perfumed. These were all attributes of Ivory, which was the only such product on the market at the time. Its long-time slogan perfectly captured that: '99 and $44/100$% Pure.' Bernays created events – a soap yacht race in New York's Central Park, soap-carving contests and plenty of others – that generated media coverage and got people talking about and using Ivory soap.

Contemporary PR practitioners might employ the same sorts of tactics today, except we'd likely use analytics to map stakeholders' points of view and everyday soap preferences, enlist the support of mom and kid bloggers, recruit other influencers, post videos of the competitions online and encourage participation that would be shared on social media.

The founders of some of the first PR agencies always viewed their discipline through a wide lens. From the earliest days, their solutions for clients were multi-dimensional and used various platforms. For instance, when David Finn and Bill Ruder started their PR agency, Ruder Finn, in 1948, they never thought of themselves as 'media' people. That early generation drew on whatever communications it needed – lobbying, advertising, influencer endorsement, media outreach, events and more.

Reading case studies and talking to seasoned professionals about what worked and didn't work can yield valuable lessons. There are many excellent sources worth checking out: online and print industry publications like *PRWeek*, *PRovoke Media*, *Ragan Communications* and *Reputation Today*. The Arthur W. Page Society, a professional association of senior comms leaders, is another excellent resource, as are various organizations and programs around the world, such as the Public Relations Society of America, the Chartered Institute of Public Relations and the *PRWeek UK* events series. The Cannes Lions Awards include a PR category. You'll find helpful links to some of these in the Resources section at the back of this book. Finally, PR agency websites often include case studies.

The recognized forefathers of our field – who, besides Bernays, Finn and Ruder, include Harold Burson, Daniel Edelman and Al Golin – brought deep skills to the practice that reflected politics and pop culture, and drew on history, psychology and philosophy to develop their successful programming. Good models, then and now.

An excellent source for the history of the discipline is The Museum of Public Relations. You'll find the link to its website in the Resources section. The site offers a rich trove of information for PR professionals at any stage in their careers. For anybody traveling to New York City, I'd recommend stopping by the museum to see the fascinating collection of artifacts and memorabilia.

"

Strong relationships are based on trust and communication. But if there is no communication, there can be no trust.

"

Simon Sinek

CHAPTER 3
CORE TENETS

For companies and brands to have positive, sustainable relationships with stakeholders, they need to be trusted. Information they release – in any form, from any source, on any platform – needs to be credible. They must have a reputation for being and doing good. In this chapter, I'll share the principles behind creating public relations narratives, strategies and programming that engage people, change minds and build relationships that endure.

TRUST

Trust is among the most important attributes we have as human beings, companies have as makers of brands they sell, and organizations have as representatives of a cause. Trust should always drive strategy, messaging, materials and channel-agnostic PR work. As such, practitioners must have trust as their professional (and personal!) North Star.

CREDIBILITY

Think about people you know who have shared information that turned out to be inaccurate or downright untrue. How did you feel when you learned what you thought was reliable, valuable information was not? Did it make you want to believe these individuals ever again?

Now translate that feeling into a business context. If a company or brand communicates information that is not well sourced, not evidence-based or wildly exaggerated, how would you feel about that company or brand?

PR practitioners are the flag-bearers of credibility. Indeed, a significant role of many PR teams is to serve as the company's social conscience, and with this comes great responsibility. In addition to shaping and amplifying a company or brand voice, it falls to PR to bring the voices of stakeholders to the table and ensure that their perspectives are heard, understood and considered. That means proactively engaging with the press, and protecting the enterprise by advocating for integrity and empathy in every interaction and communication that we touch.

STRATEGY AND INSIGHTS

Simply put, a PR strategy is the single vision that sets out how communications will achieve the stated goal. Given the tools we have available, strategies can be based on a rigorous data-driven process with input including quantitative and qualitative market research, competitive information and stakeholder conversations. Effective strategies also reflect an insight – an intuitive observation.

A classic exercise is a SWOT (Strengths, Weaknesses, Opportunities and Threats) assessment. This provides a structured way to develop ideas that are business-critical and avoid the risk of 'topic drift,' where you craft a strategy that might be interesting but doesn't address what is needed most. Try it for yourself.

EXERCISE 1: SWOT ANALYSIS

Choose a product situation.

Draw a large grid, dividing it into four equal quadrants. Label the top two 'Strengths' and 'Weaknesses', and label the bottom two quadrants 'Opportunities' and 'Threats'. Work your way through each section. Brainstorm Strengths: These will likely be internal factors, including sources, expertise or unique capabilities. Brainstorm Weaknesses: These will likely be internal factors like limitations, skills gaps or resource constraints (staffing, budget, time). Brainstorm Opportunities: These will likely be external factors you can use to your advantage (relevant news items, trends or changing customer needs/demands). Brainstorm Threats: These will likely be external factors that might challenge you (competitors, regulators, challenging economic factors.)

Now, review the outputs. Group similar points in each quadrant and identify any recurring themes or patterns. Amplify and Minimize: Brainstorm ideas that maximize/show off your Opportunities and Strengths, while developing ideas that minimize/mitigate Weaknesses and Threats.

Here's an example you can consider as you work through your own SWOT analysis grid.

SWOT ANALYSIS OF COCA-COLA

STRENGTHS	WEAKNESSES
Strong Brand Identity	Competition with Pepsi
Strong Brand Value	Product Diversification
Global Reach	Health Issues
Market Share	Infringement Lawsuits
Repositioning Portfolio	Overdependence on Third-Party Technology Providers
Brand Association	

OPPORTUNITIES	THREATS
Extension of the Ready-to-drink (RTD) Market	Water Usage Controversy
Add New Goods to the Market and Lessen Added Sugar	Pollution Lawsuit
Profits from the Declining Value of the U.S. Currency	Fierce Competition
Leveraging TikTok	Economic Uncertainty
	Increasing Health Awareness
	Possible Contamination

Source: The Business Model Analyst

REPUTATION

While always top-of-mind, reputation building and reputation management are particularly front and center in PR, as companies in both developed and emerging markets recognize the role and value of "a good name." The work of building and sustaining reputation is harder than ever due to factors like media fragmentation, growing disinformation, misinformation and lack of trust, transparency and authenticity, diversity and inclusion, and integration of technology. You'll find more on the 'hard work of a good reputation' in Chapter 12.

EXERCISE 2

List three companies or brands whose communications you trust, and indicate why.

List three companies you think have good reputations and why.

Is there any overlap between these lists?

Jot down the attributes you trust and that you feel contribute to the good reputation.

"

Inspiration is for amateurs. The rest of us just show up and get to work.

"

Chuck Close

CHAPTER 4
PR FUNDAMENTALS

Underpinning tenets – the overriding principles covered in Chapter 3 – are underlying fundamentals. There is no substitute for a healthy and steadfast dedication to skills necessary for our profession. Proficiency in the fundamentals builds confidence that sets you free creatively and intellectually, incentivizes you to keep learning, and ensures that you never get bored over the course of what I hope is your long and fruitful career in public relations.

My devotion to fundamentals is hardly unique, which is why I'm always so surprised to hear Human Resources heads and recruiters say they have noticed a drop-off in what they call a 'dedication to the fundamentals' among new applicants for PR roles.

Bill Straub, coach of the famed women's bowling team at the University of Nebraska, is known for his rigorous emphasis on fundamentals. He believes mastery of these skills is the only way to reach one's full potential. In fact, his recruitment strategy is not to tell the super-talented girls who want to bowl for him how awesome they are, and how they'll contribute to a winning team, but to instead entice them with a promise: "I will make them better, if they allow me."

Coach Straub's fundamentals drills are so intense that his critics refer to them as 'clone husking,' a play on 'cornhuskers,' the University of Nebraska's traditional nickname for its sports teams. The 'clone husking' reference to his team's uniform excellence could sound derogatory but apparently doesn't disturb Straub. I'm heartened by this response.

Mastery of PR fundamentals is no different. And it is important to realize from the start that you'll likely achieve *mastery* (with a lower case 'm') relatively quickly, but you'll practice and perfect and evolve these same skills throughout your life to get to *Mastery*. It takes work, and you'll need to be relentless about it, but it will never be boring.

A great deal of PR programming, from brand support to crisis management, is based on these elements: **strategic planning; audience segmentation; messages; 'the face' and 'voice' for the messages; a core idea; channel selection**. Contained within these elements are steps that need to be taken with care and precision.

Here is my top 10 list of must-have PR fundamentals:

1. <u>CURIOSITY</u>: Albert Einstein said, "Once you stop learning, you start dying." Learning takes place everywhere if you're present and open to it. There is no right way to do it. An active investment in learning doesn't need to be formal, although all sorts of classes and one-day programs are widely available, in-person and online. Informal, everyday opportunities abound, such as reading or exploring new neighborhoods and geographies, even within your own city. Simply talking to people and asking questions can be eye-opening, enriching and professionally valuable. Learning can also take place as a quiet activity: daydreaming, meditation and silent observation.

2. <u>MESSAGE AND MOTIVE INTEGRITY</u>: Integrity – the quality of being honest and having strong moral principles – is at the core of trust, and truly the only way to be credible. As golfers would say, you don't get many mulligans here; there are very few opportunities for do-overs once trust is compromised.

3. <u>EMPATHY</u>: Awareness of the sensibilities, opinions and perspectives of others is the bedrock of successful PR. In its purest form, empathy puts you in touch with your target audience in a way that is almost intimate. It's an extremely useful power to have in any form of communication. Scratching the surface of empathy is never enough. To be empathetic to your stakeholders, you need to study their habits and their daily activities through research: quantitative data acquired through a questionnaire of your own design or culled from existing research. Supplement that with information gleaned from online sources: blogs, message boards, articles from reliable sources and, if possible,

in-person interviews. Take care not to view the findings of your research through the prism of your own experiences, preferences or feelings if you are not representative of the target audience.

4. <u>AGILITY</u>: The *need* to move quickly – either proactively or responsively – has always been critical to effective communications. Due to the proliferation of channels and the 24/7 grind of news and content, the *need to* move quickly has driven agencies and corporate PR departments to improve, and now many are better at this than ever. Agility can be demonstrated in many ways. Understanding the communications preferences of your current and desired stakeholders will help channel your agility-readiness.

5. <u>WRITING CRISP, CLEAN, COMPLETE SENTENCES</u>: Public relations practitioners need to write all the time. We write pitches to reporters to encourage interest in the individuals, companies and brands we represent. We write invitations to events, social media posts and articles, scripts for videos, speeches and so much more. From the beginning of a campaign, we put research findings into words, present insights and showcase our ideas with memorable language. Clarity of writing is an output of clarity of thought. If you can write clear sentences, it follows that you can think them; and if you can think them, you can speak them. And then, it follows that you will be more confident and effective as a communicator. The way to strengthen one's ability to write is to practice, practice, practice. And read.

EXERCISE 3

Imagine you are the PR representative of a company launching a new fitness app. You want reporters to interview the company CEOs so the offering can be presented as innovative and will disrupt the market. Write customized, five-sentence media pitches targeting specific beat reporters. Write one intended for a health reporter. Now, write a second pitch customized for a tech reporter. Then, craft one that will get the attention of a lifestyle features writer.

6. <u>COLLABORATION</u>: Working as a team makes everyone, and all your output, stronger. There are many aspects to developing this ability. Here are three important ones:

> *Identify your own strengths*
  Dr. Martin Seligman, Director of the University of Pennsylvania's Positive Psychology Center, suggests a series of exercises to help people identify their signature strength. Among these is the following exercise:

EXERCISE 4

Think of an anecdote from a time when you were at your best. It doesn't need to be a life-changing event, but should have a clear beginning, middle and end. Write a brief account of the occasion and re-read it every day for a week. Each time, ask yourself:

* What strengths did I display when I was at my best?
* Did I show creativity? Good judgment?
* Was I supportive of other people?

Writing down your answers to such self-reflective questions puts you in touch with what you're good at. Then, think about how to use these strengths to your advantage.

> *Connect*

The 2017 Future of Work report from management consultancy Deloitte found that 65% of C-Level executives surveyed had a strategic objective to transform their organization's culture, with a focus on connectivity, communication and collaboration. The ability to collaborate is the holy grail of every work environment. It is also key to a successful agency/client relationship. To be sure, it is possible to use technology to collaborate via shared files, group emails, Zoom or Teams sessions. We've all gotten used to working successfully remotely, all the more so since COVID-19 lockdowns. But actual face-to-face human connection makes a real difference. There is no substitute for eye contact, the ability to recognize a change in tone in reaction to an idea, or read another's body language.

> *Be helpful and helpable*

Take and give constructive support. Sometimes this feels like, and is indeed, criticism. Remembering that criticism makes you and your work stronger can take the sting out, whether you are on the giving or receiving end.

7. __EMBRACE NEW TECHNOLOGY__: PR practitioners need to be able to read, understand and interpret data and use advanced analytics tools. AI is already changing communications. We now have access to incredible amounts of data that allow us to predict target audiences' preferences and behavior. An abundance of easily accessible tools help capture data that are directly actionable for PR. Using AI, PR professionals can also test their ideas and the channels they use. For example, if a company decides to create a stand-alone website to support an issue, it is easy and inexpensive, from an IT cost and people resource perspective, to build a relatively thin site and make it available to the target audience. If data demonstrates that the messaging has resonated, then it makes sense to add to it. Similarly, data reflects whether an activity should be scaled down. These predictive analytics and algorithms bring certainty to the process.

New generative AI solutions are added to the PR toolbox all the time. I have my own favorites, but by the time you read this they may all be replaced by newer, better, faster options. The best thing to do is seek advice from the experts (see Chapter 11) and always research reviews of the latest tools. Many are available free of charge.

8. <u>STORYTELLING</u>: There is a growing body of scientific data revealing how the brain reacts when 'on story'. This is a phrase I learned from Brent McCallum, who heads up Make Believe, a storytelling agency. When your brain is on story, it is actively engaged and aware. In PR, stories are the guiding light for building company or product brands. A storyline creates strategic clarity, broad alignment and a sense of shared purpose, helping organizations move further and faster, with internal and external stakeholders.

When developing company or brand narratives, I often look to favorite authors for inspiration. Anton Chekhov is a top choice for many reasons, but chiefly because he laid down six principles that make for a good story. If they were good enough for this influential literary figure, they are good enough for me. Here they are:

1. Absence of lengthy verbiage
2. Total objectivity
3. Truthful descriptions
4. Extreme brevity
5. Audacity and originality ('flee the stereotype')
6. Compassion

For more on these principles, or if you would like to read about Chekov, you can check out *The Letters of Anton Chekhov* online. While you're at it, read his wonderful short stories.

EXERCISE 5: SIX-WORD STORIES

Write a complete story (happy or sad) in six words.

A famously poignant piece of 'flash fiction' that's attributed to Ernest Hemingway goes like this: "For sale: baby shoes, never worn." How powerful is that?

9. <u>MEASUREMENT</u>. If I had a penny for every discussion I've had, or article I've read, on how to measure PR, I'd be rich. Oh, the hand-wringing that has gone into the return on investment (ROI) for PR versus, say, paid advertising on any channel – whether mobile, social, print, outdoor or broadcast, all of which are associated with a 'hard' return. While both disciplines are responsible for creating relationships of a sort, advertising is based on creating a revenue-producing relationship with stakeholders. PR can certainly achieve this, but that is not its sole purpose.

"The R in PR doesn't stand for revenue," Jon Iwata, former Chief Communications Officer of IBM, once told me in an interview. That said, PR is highly successful at enhancing awareness, driving first-time trial experience, forging brand loyalty and creating brand preference, all of which positively impact revenue.

The relationships created by PR have been considered difficult to measure and hard to directly link to sales. This is less the case today when data can make a direct connection. However, because of this perception, PR is sometimes relegated to the 'nice to have' column rather than the 'must have.' I can think of three occasions off the top of my head when I lost 90% of my PR budget to advertising due to that misperception. I'll never forget when Adam, a client – with whom we have a particularly strong relationship – cut our hard-won budget to a fraction. That he delivered this news on my birthday made the disappointment unforgettable. He was apologetic, but explained that he needed to generate a short-term sales boost. While frustrating, we shifted our recommendations to support the ad campaign, built back our budget over time, and I'm happy to say that Adam is still our client today.

Our ability to measure the value of PR to a business or a brand has been enhanced by data. A variety of services we can employ now enable PR to test, validate and then measure the effectiveness of our messaging and the activities we implement. For comprehensive campaigns, such as a product launch, it is still best to apply the appropriate measures to every element of an integrated effort, as it is the collective performance that will drive the outcome.

10. <u>ON BEING AN 'EXPERT'</u>: As a life-long learner, this is a thing for me: while I have *expertise*, I never present myself as an *expert* on the basis that it suggests I have nothing else to learn. Many persuasive reasons exist for perceiving yourself as a *novice*. For instance, it prevents complacency and keeps you hungry. I'll leave you with my favorite quotation from the screenwriter William Goldman, who famously said, "Nobody knows anything."

"

If you change the way you look at things, the things you look at change.

"

Wayne Dyer

CHAPTER 5
THINK ATTRACTION, NOT PROMOTION

If PR is about making connections and changing minds, this requires a *two-way* relationship.

Therein lies a critical insight about 'promotion', a role PR is often called in for, and the difference between promotion and attraction.

Promotion is one-way communication, a 'push' of information via one channel or a collection of them. It is essentially a demand to be heard and seen. From the perspective of the target audience, it is a receipt of information, wanted or unwanted.

Viewed positively, promotion can inspire curiosity. It creates awareness. It makes an offer. Promotion can also provoke an action, whether information-seeking or something more.

Conversely, promotion asks for stakeholder time, attention and consideration without regard to their schedule, need or likelihood of interest. As a result, promotion can be considered irritating. Invasive. Unsolicited. Something to be ignored.

Attraction is different. Attraction is *mutual* – a joint desire to connect, and an appetite for information. When the attraction is there, receipt of information feels more like a natural flow than a barrage.

Additionally, attraction operates on a different rhythm than promotion. It feels friendlier, more relaxed. It doesn't come with either the volume or the urgency of promotion. If orchestrated effectively, it can almost feel inevitable.

Elliot Sloane, who founded corporate and investor relations firm Sloane Communications, gave me the powerful illustration of the difference between attraction and promotion the day after seeing the band U2 at the Joshua Tree concert in New York City.

> Bono (the band's singer) is a total rock star. It's funny how that whole vibe he gives off, that glow he radiates that is so irresistible, reminds me of (business magnate and financier) T. Boone Pickens. I worked for Boone for years. My firm was involved in and managed all the earned media for his Pickens Plan. Our goal was to communicate the benefits of getting the US off foreign oil and onto our own resources – wind, solar, natural gas. I got to know Boone very well during this assignment. He's an incredible guy. Smart. Charismatic. Tireless. A real leader. From humble roots. Boone is the kind of guy who commands the spotlight. Who generates heat by just standing there. Like Bono.

> As Boone's PR guy, I used to marvel at how much the mainstream press – I mean the largest and most complex and hardest-to-work-with press – all wanted to talk to him. The sell wasn't in getting the press interested. They were always interested. The work was in figuring out how to choreograph, how to strategize, how to emerge with the results we wanted. I used to tell people, without ever having met Bono or even without ever having seen him in concert, that working for Boone was like working for Bono.

A pure rock star. A guy who turned heads standing still. Last night, watching Bono perform, there was the difference between attraction and promotion in action. There was Bono, in his black outfit, his tinted glasses, standing all alone on an extended stage, his band members a few hundred feet behind him ... standing all alone, holding his mic, not just standing in his rock star pose, but being a rock star. With his own manner of humility and intellect, attracting his audience, not promoting to it. The emotional buy-in when there's this kind of attraction is incredible. Not surprising, but incredible.

Promotion, or being promoted, is far less likely to give you this feeling.

When you focus on creating an attraction among stakeholders to your message, your actions and your initiatives, you've shifted the goal posts. And in doing so, added energy and excitement.

Focusing on attraction opens up new avenues for communication. It frees you to find authentic connections and sources of influence. These add a vibrancy to the creative process that amps up the passion. Try it, and let me know how it goes for you.

Anyone can have a megaphone. Getting heard and having that message resonate is something else altogether.

HOW TO CREATE ATTRACTION

- First, do your homework to get to know your stakeholder audience. How do they spend their time? What are their everyday challenges and needs as they relate to your brand? What gives them pleasure? What frustrates them? Who are their 'rock stars?'

- Once you know your stakeholders, you can find meaningful intersections for your brand or message at key moments in their everyday lives – times when they'd find the brand messages most attractive. Data can help.

- Then, look for a driver insight – something universal to all stakeholders, ideally, that will serve as the core of your campaign. Build the language and images around that insight that will create positive connections for them to your message, making stakeholders feel as if your brand is speaking directly to them.

- Consider the tactics that could bring the insight to life and encourage people to engage in real life and online.

Consumers need some sense that a company or a brand knows them and cares about them and their needs, challenges and aspirations, and is delivering on those essentials. This approach creates attraction because it requires stakeholders to allow your message, brand or company into their lives, versus promotion, which is just in their faces.

EXERCISE 6: CREATE ATTRACTION

Here's the brand challenge: A pharmaceutical company wants to reach a diverse audience aged 45+ about the importance of knowing their risks of developing heart disease. This includes encouraging people to know their blood pressure, cholesterol and triglyceride numbers, and understand the connection between body weight and cardiac health. Your job is to understand the audiences, put yourself in their shoes and identify the best ways to attract them to your message. Think about this challenge, and begin by asking yourself the following questions:

- What sources of information do your stakeholders trust when it comes to their health?
- Where does your target audience spend time? We once held a heart-healthy screening in a place called the 'World's Largest Laundromat' in Chicago – a non-traditional venue to say the least, but the hub of the local Hispanic community, which was the target audience.
- What are their sources of discontent or areas of frustration about health?
- Who are their role models?
- Does your audience need something that takes their mind off an issue or situation that concerns them? In that case, perhaps your role in the relationship is to be the source of a welcome distraction.
- Do your stakeholders feel 'heard?'

The aim of PR messaging and engagement based on attraction is to convert passive stakeholders into active ones who invite you and want you and your brand in their lives. They see how your messages and opportunities benefit them. They want to hear and really listen. They want to participate and engage. And finally, they want to pursue what they've learned – they're anxious to try the brand – and share what they've learned with family, friends, colleagues and others in their world.

CHAPTER 6
THINK MEANINGFUL, NOT JUST 'SNACKABLE,' CONTENT

I was once in three client meetings over a single week where the discussion was whether the content we were developing about a chronic disease and a biomedical R&D topic needed to be 'snackable.' Short. Punchy. Pithy. 'Two-bite.' Was brevity necessary to capture the ever-shortening stakeholder attention span?

Ever since the infamous 'goldfish study' released by Microsoft in 2015 – which asserted that people had an eight-second attention span, which was shorter than the nine-second threshold of a goldfish – communicators, marketers and some C-Suite leaders have believed stakeholders will get distracted or tune out if a message or piece of content isn't both compelling and delivered super quickly. The other assumption is that we'd need quantity – hit our audiences multiple times with the same briefly delivered message – for the information to stick.

It is clear human attention spans are changing. Look no further than the rise of TikTok, with its videos averaging just 35 seconds in duration, and our attachment to multi-tasking. Indeed, a study from the Neuroleadership Institute found that 93% of people say they can multi-task as well as, or better than, the average person.

But as storytellers and communicators of valuable information that we want our target stakeholders to use, learn and benefit from, and – finally – act on, is aiming for a seconds-long scrap of attention effective or even necessary?

The science says no.

I'm trained to rely on research, data and proof points when we develop narratives – what I've recently started to call the narrative mosaic – for client content. I also can't resist relatable anecdotal evidence. Consider the following:

- Humans have the capacity to pay attention to things for long periods of time. Moreover, there's no real evidence that attention spans have declined.

- It takes longer than seconds to 'memory encode.' This is how information coming from content gets changed into a form that can be stored in the brain, processed and placed in categories for mental storage and retrieval. Content that 'memory encodes' tends to stick.

- Immersive storytelling releases oxytocin, the so-called 'love hormone,' in our brains, which triggers our emotional centers, enabling us to connect to the content. This happens because our curiosity becomes unlocked. We're interested, drawn in. When more of our brains are engaged, we pay attention for longer, we care, we remember, we repeat.

- And, finally, who among us hasn't binge-watched a television show? I confess, not without a little shame, that on a recent weekend I found myself with the apartment and the remote to myself, binge-watching two seasons – 11 straight hours! – of the Netflix series, '*Emily in Paris.*'

What do all these findings mean? With a well-told, informative narrative, it is possible to capture and keep stakeholder attention for minutes, rather than seconds, and achieve, if not exceed, communications objectives.

Here are five approaches to consider:

1. Plan content for a variety of attention types: arousal (alertness); focused (paying attention); selective (the ability to attend to a specific stimulus or activity in the presence of another, as in watching a TikTok while reading something); and sustained, with focused attention over a longer period, when you want stakeholders to be *all in*.

2. Know which platforms your stakeholders prefer, and when in the day they're like to engage. Then, plan the length of content that will capture their attention in the most effective way, on the optimal platform, at the right moments.

3. Serialize the content. This approach is the best of both worlds, allowing you to utilize immersive storytelling in smaller, digestible parts over time. We took this approach in an assignment to create an immersive narrative mosaic for the R&D 'triple threat' – strategy, team and science – of a multinational biopharma company. A key element of our solution centered on podcast serials that

broke down one story into consumable, 26–30-minute portions that were both individually compelling and worked together to give rise to a whole that was greater than the sum of its parts. The podcast serials attracted tens of thousands of internal and external stakeholders, who returned for the next episode and the next series. The program grew to include companion webinars, bylined articles, social media and a refreshed microsite.

4. Use brief, seconds-long content to drive your audience to longer-form content. Here, think quick snapshots on social media that lead to articles on the organization's website.

5. Surprise! The unexpected triggers emotional reactions – excitement, joy, curiosity – that make stakeholders feel invested. To reach our target audience for the PeriCoach, a solution for women suffering from urinary incontinence, we took an unexpected path: humor. A centerpiece two-and-a-half-minute video we called 'Leakers Anonymous' carried a warning: 'This video will cause laughter.' Leakers, for whom a belly-laugh (or sneezing, coughing or sudden exertion) can cause a urinary event, prepare yourself before watching! Viewers – women and healthcare professionals – were drawn into the longer-than-usual story. They laughed. They cried. They commiserated. Most importantly, they took action: we were able to measure an uptick in information-seeking and sales.

An article in the October 2023 issue of *Harvard Business Review* offers six rules that business leaders should follow to create stories that work: convey authenticity; feature yourself; break with the past and lay a path to the future; appeal to hearts and minds; be theatrical; empower others. Being 'snackable' is not required.

"

Logic will get you from A to B. Imagination will take you everywhere.

"

Albert Einstein

CHAPTER 7
CREATIVITY

PR has a rich heritage of clever campaigns that result in better, stronger connections to a company or brand's stakeholders. Sometimes these involved an unexpected exploitation of a competitor's weakness, or an insight that had been hidden in plain sight.

Creativity, especially in service of building reputation, takes work. You can find originality, a truly imaginative idea, if you're honest and unfiltered. As a reality check, I also keep in mind what stand-up comedian Bo Burnham says: "Original doesn't mean good." Just saying.

A PR CREATIVE EFFORT NEEDS TO BE EFFECTIVE

Creativity in PR business terms needs to be grounded in a business objective with performance metrics. Creativity needs to move the brand, move the company, in some way, and get it closer to meeting the stated goals and objectives.

That said, finding creative PR solutions is fun work. It requires risk-taking and a concerted effort to identify and think through a new idea, make it work and sell it up the line. Will your internal and external audiences get it? Will it convince customers to choose this brand?

Or, in the case of a healthcare brand – the space I work in – ask their doctor about it? Coming up with a creative idea requires far more human resources than buying more advertising in a different medium, developing coupons or offering free trials.

Campaigns that generate buzz, change behavior or become models in the industry typically center on a creative idea or creative execution of a brand insight. Creativity breaks the mold, taking us to places we didn't think possible. Creativity is exciting.

According to a survey of agency and client executives conducted for the OMD media agency network by *Ad Age* and Erdos & Morgan, creativity tops the list of qualities clients look for in media agencies. That's followed closely by data and analytics, and efficient business processes. While creativity is at the top, these numbers reveal the tightrope that marketers are walking between a desire for innovation and the determination to win.

To get your creative juices flowing, here are a few suggestions:

- Identify which brands and circumstances would benefit most from a creative idea or solution.

- Stay open-minded when it comes to customer desires or unmet needs. Respect, but do not be restricted by, market research, keeping in mind what Henry Ford said: "If I asked my customers what they wanted, they'd have said a faster horse."

- Focus your creativity on solving a discontent. As comedian Jerry Seinfeld says, "What am I really sick of?" This is a good starting point for innovative thinking.

- Demand creativity, creative thinking and creative solutions of your teams and from your agencies.

- Find a balance of creativity and business objectives within your overall brand strategies.

In the 1990s, senior marketers at the Swedish vodka brand Absolut, a long time client of my jacobstahl partner, Jeremy, used to debate whether the company's advertising campaign, widely recognized as among the most enduring and transformative, was a case of creativity trumping strategy. Absolut's ads centered around its distinctively-shaped bottle and always included a tagline that said 'Absolut [Something]' — 'Absolut Perfection,' or a flavor, as in 'Absolut Mandarin,' or a theme often focused on art ('Absolut Haring' and 'Absolut Warhol'), or a fashion reference. It also extended to cities ('Absolut L.A.'). This simplicity was revolutionary, allowing for endless creative iterations while maintaining brand recognition. Despite the never-ending debate (creativity versus strategy), who can argue with the success of the brand or the campaign?

Consider the approach the American insurance company Blue Cross Blue Shield of North Carolina took when it embarked on the integrated 'scapegoat' campaign, designed to position itself and the health insurance industry as part of *the solution*. The grassroots effort featured a mascot – a real goat! – that made appearances at farmer's markets, business meetings and sporting events. Web advertising, PR and print ads rounded out the mix.

You can also look to the decades-long, still running 'Real Beauty' campaigns from skincare giant Dove. One of the more recent iterations is The *#NoDigitalDistortion*. This is an initiative, targeted to teens and designed to build confidence and body-positivity, and included a *Confidence Kit* of self-esteem-building tips and expert advice, and encouraged adults to have a 'Selfie Talk' with a young person to build perspective and resilience.

There are many ways to achieve your goals. Market research, analytics and a tight strategy all have their places as 'must haves,' alongside creativity.

"Ideas never come out fully formed," says Mark Zuckerberg, founder and CEO of Meta Platforms, inc. "They become so over time, as you work on them."

Here are some suggestions to cultivate your creativity:

- Do something creative for two minutes as soon as you wake up in the morning. Produce some kind of output: write a few lines, compose a melody, jot down an idea for a lyric, sing an original song in the shower.

- If not first thing in the morning, schedule a few minutes each day to write. Carl Richards, author of *Want to be Creative on Purpose? Schedule It*, notes that this is the exact opposite of waiting for inspiration to strike.

- Find inspirations. They're around you if you're open to spotting them and then allowing them in.

- Find quiet time. The inventor Nikola Tesla believed that being alone was the secret of invention. "That," he said, "is when ideas are born."

- Do nothing. The psychologist, and hero of mine, Amos Tversky had his own version of this point: "The secret to doing good research is always to be a little underemployed."

EXERCISE 7: THIRTY CIRCLES

The design and innovation agency IDEO came up with The *Thirty Circles Challenge*, a useful creativity icebreaker. Using the collection of circles below, draw a recognizable object in each of them, completing the entire exercise in three minutes. Time yourself. How many circles did you complete?

Are there recognizable patterns or are any of your ideas related? Did you 'break the rules' by combining circles, or use them in an unexpected way? This can be a great exercise for visualizing ideas and thinking outside the box (circle!). Do it yourself, or try it in a brainstorming session or team meeting.

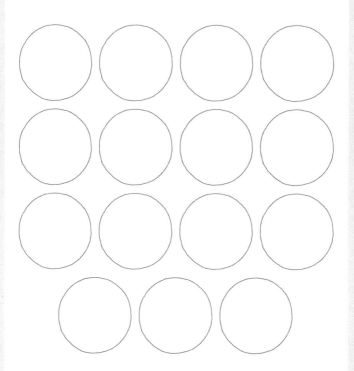

If the idea is evidence-based and can truly be supported, it is often up to the public relations people to step up and offer a solution or an approach that is new, unexpected, and at the very least will get people thinking differently.

Finally, I like to foster a little restlessness in myself, my teams at work and my students when thinking through creative ideas. Sometimes a great idea may be ahead of its time for a client, and is put aside, assuming it will be difficult (if not impossible) to sell. In these cases, I like to think 'no' is just the first two letters of 'not yet.'

"

Most people do not listen with the intent to understand; they listen with the intent to reply.

"

Stephen R. Covey

CHAPTER 8
LISTEN

For about four years, I worked as Vice President of Marketing Communications and PR for a start-up oncology diagnostics company. Every month, the management team would meet at 9am for a daylong state-of-the-business session. Inevitably, by 10:30am (or noon, tops), it would become a free-for-all. It was difficult to finish a sentence, let alone get through a presentation, without someone interrupting to agree, disagree, build on the thought or bring up a point that was perhaps related, but on a different track. We all kind of got used to this and just rolled with the flow. That was the culture of this company. But when a new COO joined – a Canadian who had just completed a stint at a multinational – he was appalled at the raucousness of these meetings. And he said so. He quickly banned interrupting and the discussions became more disciplined, though it resulted in people holding back. Meetings were more orderly but not as much creativity or problem-solving took place.

Listening – I mean really listening – and actually hearing each other shouldn't be so difficult. But it is, and it takes work. Listening requires a pause, taking a step back before responding. This enables the listener to understand why stakeholders feel and act the way they do.

In his book, *On Becoming a Person*, psychologist Carl Rogers wrote, "Real communication occurs when we listen with understanding

– to see the idea and attitude from the other person's point of view, to sense how it feels to them, to achieve their frame of reference in regard to the thing they are talking about."

LISTEN MORE THAN YOU TALK

Active listening is a key element of creating connections. Today, we can listen in may ways – through AI and predictive analytics, the news, surveys, as well as the old-school 'ears to the ground' that comes from strong relationships. With this knowledge, communicators can understand what matters most.

The balance should be 10% speaking and 90% listening. This sage sage advice has been around for many thousands of years. Indeed, Zeno of Citium, a Hellenistic thinker from 336–265 BCE, was known to have said, "We have two ears and one mouth, so we should listen more than we say." As if it were that simple. But it is more worthwhile to do so than not. The benefits can be surprising.

LISTENING FOR COLLABORATION AND INNOVATION

Henry Elkus, CEO of Helena, a non-profit organization that convenes world leaders to discuss and implement solutions to global issues, views internal management meetings differently than the COO at my start-up. Elkus creates the kind of environment in which it is possible to hear feedback from everyone in his company. As a result of this openness, one of Helena's interns helped dramatically improve the direction his organization would take. "The intern saved me and the rest of our team the wasted time and energy we might have spent continuing down a suboptimal path," Elkus said.

> **"June Rokoff, Senior VP for Software Development at Lotus, credits her success in turning around the company's position in the software industry to building a team that listens. She made listening the culture of her team."**
>
> Glen Rifkin

LISTEN TO STAKEHOLDERS

Internal PR departments, often along with their agencies, are expected to be the eyes and ears of their companies. Our backgrounds and training often establish PR professionals as the most qualified to serve in this role, and advise company leadership accordingly. This skill is needed on an ongoing basis, but never more than when stakeholders do not agree with the company's message or a particular action. This is the only way to understand the *why* behind their point of view, and use the insights gleaned to chart the communications course.

Listening allows companies to find common ground with critics. It's often possible to devise a PR strategy that shines a spotlight on those areas of agreement, while on a parallel track the company works to address areas of disconnect or discontent.

LISTENING, IN EVERY WAY

There are many ways to listen in live interactions, including in person, on the phone or via videochats. Less talking and closer attention allows you to absorb and assess what people say – the words they use, their tone of voice, their body language, their overall demeanor and presentation. I'm reminded here of a court stenographer I once hired to attend a symposium we'd organized for a client and deliver a detailed transcript of the presentations. To my surprise, she was profoundly hearing-impaired! She did her job, and an excellent one at that, through lip-reading and observations derived from her heightened alternate senses.

Technology also provides us with a variety of tools and services to help capture listening information more efficiently. Social listening has given us listening scale as well as depth.

'RESILIENT' LISTENING

Listening means inviting people to speak, and then actually hearing and taking in a variety of points of view that reflect different experiences, contributing factors and perspectives. This is hard, and getting harder as people become more segmented and everyday issues become more polarizing. Now multiply by ten the difficulty of respectfully taking in different viewpoints on a highly charged, deeply contentious topic, and you've got 'resilient listening.' Mastering this skill can create the environment for conflicting perspectives to be shared so that a foundation for moving forward can be honestly considered.

"

I don't think we're really listening unless we're willing to be changed by the other person.

"

Alan Alda

LISTENING FOR INCLUSION

Trust and social responsibility, longtime stalwarts of communications, are in the spotlight. Exceptional attention needs to be paid. Rajeev Chawla, Course Head of Public Relations and Corporate Communications at Xavier Institute of Communications in Mumbai, puts it this way, "Companies are getting and exhibiting their souls now. Communications plays a significant role."

Companies lose employees and stakeholders when they don't feel seen or heard, or sense that they don't have a valuable voice. It's not enough to invite them in and ask what they think. They need to perceive that their opinions and points of view legitimately matter. It is not possible to overstate the benefits of listening for inclusion.

Listening and really hearing lets in all points of view and helps ensure that they land on a receptive audience, are considered and truly contribute to the communications solution. This may be oriented toward the company culture, if internally-focused listening, or to messaging if externally facing. This process should not feel like a struggle. It should be natural and organic and moving forward. Based on my experience with Millennials, I am confident it will be.

Want to improve your listening? Emma Seppälä, Ph.D., Science Director of Stanford University's Center for Compassion and Altruism Research and Education, and the author of *The Happiness Track*, and Jennifer Steven, VP of Client Services and Faculty at TLEX (Transformational Leadership for Excellence) Institute, have these suggestions for active listening:

- Be genuinely curious and interested in what is being said, even if initially you're not.

- Pay attention to cues: Does the person spend a lot of time on a particular point?

- Ask yourself whether they get more animated at specific junctures and less so at others.

Listening more, and with true curiosity, not only helps you to better connect and understand what is being said, but also provides valuable input on how you may frame your response and navigate the conversation. It can help you tune into the topics the other person is passionate about. Getting to know them will help you see their perspective and come to an agreement that meets everyone's needs. An excellent article about listening can be found in *Harvard Business Review*. You'll find the link in the Resources section.

EXERCISE 8

Imagine a well-known personality, or even an everyday person you think of as a good listener.

Make note of their personality, traits and attitude.

Think of a time when they demonstrated their ability to really listen and, in doing so, provided a solution or happy ending. Write down what happened.

Now, imagine yourself as the chosen person. Would you have listened as closely?

What would you do differently next time?

Write down everything that comes to mind.

_____

_____

_____

_____

_____

"

Words are loaded pistols.

"

Jean-Paul Sartre

CHAPTER 9
WORDS ARE OUR CURRENCY

That old adage about a picture being worth a thousand words is often true. Picture an expression on someone's face – for instance, a politician caught on camera in a compromising position. There are many situations in which seeing is believing. This idea reminds me of the expression, 'The best PR is being caught (literally, visually) in the act of doing something good.'

That said, words are incredibly powerful, whether spoken or written. They make strong and lasting impressions on the listener or the reader, both in everyday life and professionally.

Consider this situation: A PR friend recently told me a story about when she worked with a physician spokesperson on a media tour, intended to share data about a new cancer medication. After a great deal of planning, pitching and reference-providing, she finally scored a slot for the doctor on a much-coveted national news show. To prepare for the interview, the PR team took the physician through extensive training, anticipating as many questions as possible, and removing all the 'umms' and unnecessary gesticulations from this expert's presentation style.

During the interview, which was broadcast live, the doctor was asked whether the medication extended a patient's life, a question that had been covered in the media training. Yet, on live TV, when it was heard by millions, she said, "I can't speak to that, but I suppose everybody needs to die someday."

Mic drop. And then, silence.

This was decidedly *not* the answer she had prepared and practiced, and not something anybody expected to fly from her lips. And those last five words – which probably took up four seconds in an otherwise articulate, professionally delivered, highly valuable interview – were all anybody remembered. And not for a good reason.

Words matter. They always have. Always will.

AVOID JARGON

Every industry has a set of vocabulary, or jargon, associated with it. Typically, people outside that particular space have no idea what the terminology means, and this can result in frustration, with the audience tuning out or immediately hitting the 'delete' button. Here is a good example of jargon at its worst, posted on LinkedIn:

> "I received an email from a company that plans pay-for-play conferences, and they want access to our clients as an audience (revenue) for their events. I usually just delete those, but for some reason I replied to this one. It went like this: Me: 'Can you tell me who you are and what you do?' Him: 'We provide a platform for market-moving dialogue by connecting decision makers through actionable exchange, revolutionizing the way 21st century companies create value. When can we talk?'"

Any idea what the offer was? Me neither.

While there are always 'it' words, buzzy terms that seem to catch on and find resonance, and it totally makes sense to note them, we should use them sparingly. They'll inevitably get overused and eventually become hackneyed phrases, to the point that their meaning is anyone's guess. And their value is negligible.

It is fine to invent a new word or turn-of-phrase you can associate with a brand or company (more on this below), but otherwise, I advise use of clean language, well-chosen words and simple, well-articulated messaging.

DEVELOP A LEXICON WHEN YOU HAVE THE OPPORTUNITY

Advertising is often credited with creating new vocabulary about a particular brand or topic. Snappy copy, memorable taglines and lots of repetition contribute to this success becoming successful. How often have you used the phrase 'Just do it' for virtually any effort where a little extra motivation is needed? (Well done, Nike!) We all have our favorites. But PR can also play a critical role in establishing a new lexicon through well-placed and timed media coverage, everyday engagement and effective campaigns.

Consider a few examples from my healthcare space. There are disease states that many feel are too 'private' to name. Or, there's not a lot of available vocabulary that they're comfortable with, such as vaginal atrophy or erectile dysfunction. Or perhaps a condition is hard to say (chikungunya, a mosquito-borne disease), or is misunderstood (high triglycerides) because it is overshadowed by a more established condition (high cholesterol). What about illnesses that may have a stigma attached to them (depression)? Some highly treatable health problems go untreated because patients and their families or caregivers don't have the words to describe the symptoms. Developing vocabulary people can use, and then gently but effectively easing it into everyday vernacular and circumstances, can make the difference between silent suffering and productive action.

Well-conceived and executed PR has contributed to the successful introduction and use of socially acceptable language for a variety of situations. Considering the growing importance of stakeholder segmentation, it's safe to say that no one vocabulary fits all.

Geographic, socio-economic, cultural and demographic differences will dictate the words to use that will best communicate about an issue or brand to particular stakeholders. PR has the flexibility and the tactical arsenal to make a new lexicon about a difficult subject relatable, no matter where the target audience sits. But, that's only true if we have the words.

WORDS THAT RESONATE WITH STAKEHOLDERS

Words and phrases can trigger emotions. Different meanings and feelings can be attributed to words depending on a variety of factors, such as geography, age, culture (popular or traditional) or point of reference. In building relationships with stakeholders, you need to be aware of these factors to determine the words that will land best.

GOOD WORDS ARE EVERYWHERE

Words are all around us. You find them in newspapers and magazines, online, in social media, on billboards, in your emails and in books, new and old.

Reading is an excellent way to learn new words and turns of phrase. I'll never forget a *60 Minutes* interview I saw with the rapper Eminem in which he told journalist Anderson Cooper that he regularly reads the dictionary to find ways to rhyme. He writes down words he learns and thinks of this as 'stacking ammo.' Maybe he was thinking of Sartre ("Words are loaded pistols") when he made that statement? My favorite part was when he said he couldn't understand why people think you can't find a rhyme for the word orange. He suggested breaking the word into two syllables – *'or-inge'* – and proceeded to freestyle a string of examples: "I put my orange four-inch door hinge in storage and ate porridge with George." (You can find the YouTube link to the Eminem piece in the Resources section.)

The point he's making is that words are there for the taking. They can be found and learned and, most importantly, used to your benefit, to advance your cause and make your point, when and where you need them.

Feel free to read the dictionary like Eminem. It has always been a fantastic and super-accessible resource. I do not necessarily sit down and spend an hour reading the dictionary, but have always had one next to my computer at every desk I've ever sat at. I also use the online version at *dictionary.com*.

If spending time with dictionaries is not your thing, then simply get into the habit of writing down words that catch your attention. When you spot one, look it up. Jot it down. Try it out on your own, in speaking and in writing. Note the way it lands on an audience. If it does so positively, use it again.

EXERCISE 9

Write down five words you find interesting for any reason.
You may use them a lot yourself and like the way they
sound, perhaps you heard them from someone you admire,
or you've read them in the paper or a book. Now, have some
fun with them. Jot down a sentence using one of the words.
Write a headline with another one. Play a version of 'the
Eminem game' and write a haiku with one or more – three
lines, with five syllables in the first line, seven in the second,
five in the third.

Listen carefully to the way people you admire speak. Write down those words and phrases of theirs that you like, that resonate, that you remember well. After a couple of weeks in her first internship at a PR agency, one of my students said she loved the way her boss articulated an idea, even though she wasn't familiar with some of the words he used. I encouraged her to record these on her smartphone as soon as she heard them and then look them up later. Once she began doing this regularly, her comprehension improved, as did her vocabulary. Another benefit: she had even more admiration for her boss than she did before.

I first got into this habit myself as an account executive at global communications agency Ruder Finn. David Finn, the CEO at the time and long considered a pioneer in PR, used some rich and colorful words and phrases, several of which I still like and use. A particular favorite is 'cacophony' a word to convey when tactics or messages don't work well together, as in a symphony. Here's how I once used this idea in an article I wrote for a leading pharma marketing magazine:

> *The CEO of a company I once worked for defined success-ful campaign integration as a symphony – a confluence of several different instruments being played simultaneously by accomplished musicians, yet each instrument enhances the other resulting in moving and memorable music. When, on the other hand, those same musicians play their instruments just as skillfully, at the same time but individually, the result is a discordant cacophony.*

Make an effort to grow your vocabulary. This is a daily practice. Kind of like yoga. I promise, it never gets old.

Reading is my favorite way to build vocabulary that improves writing and the ability to articulate ideas. Here are a few games that revolve around the use of words, and are fun:

SCRABBLE®: Play this classic word game with a hardcopy dictionary, or your phone with the dictionary app, close by.

HANGMAN: This was always my go-to game when my children were young and fidgety, especially in stalled New York City subways. The Surrealists who invented it originally called it 'The Exquisite Corpse.' This is a simple word game with two players where the goal is to find the missing word or words by guessing letters before the 'hangmans' body is complete. Player 1 thinks of a word and draws a row of dashes each representing a letter of a word. Player 2 guesses one letter at a time until it's complete. With every incorrect guess, Player 1 draws another part of a body (head, arms, legs, fingers, etc.).

BANANAGRAMS®: A great game that is easy to transport and it comes in a yellow banana-shaped bag.

<u>DIVIDE QUOTES</u>: I am pretty sure I learned this game at a family Thanksgiving. Since then, I've introduced it to students in my classes. It's a great way to trot out interesting turns of phrase. For this game, I research famous quotations and then divide each into two separate parts, which I write on individual slips of paper. I fold up each slip, put them all in a cup and shake them up. Then, each person selects a slip. The first person announces their phrase, and it's up to the holders of the remaining slips to figure out if the phrase they have completes the one announced. Proceed around the room until all the quotations are complete.

EXERCISE 10: RANDOM WORD ASSOCIATION

Remember that fitness app you were pitching to a reporter in Exercise 3? Now, your challenge is to get 100 people to post short videos of their real-world experience with it on their own social media platform, and tag your brand #fitnessapp.

Choose 3–4 key words associated with this challenge.

Here are a few thought-starters. Feel free to use these or add your own.

- Attract
- Persuade
- Inspire
- Share

Then, free-associate. Taking each keyword, brainstorm random words you associate with it until you have a list of 5–10.

For each association, try to expand it into an idea.

Repeat the process: Move on to one of your other keywords. Use the new word as a fresh stimulus to generate additional ideas and associations.

"

I've learned that people will forget what you said, people will forget what you did, but people will never forget how you made them feel.

"

Maya Angelou

CHAPTER 10
CALL TO ACTION

I tend to actually make good on my New Year's Resolutions in May and early June – half a year later. This is in large part because the internet and my social feeds become filled with YouTube videos of speeches from university commencements during those months. The inspiration I feel from these can turn even my loftiest (long-deferred) aspirations into action.

Among the many powerful, charismatic speakers who emerge in these springtime graduation rituals, some really stand out. Admiral William H. McRaven, who delivered his 2014 'Make your bed' address at the University of Texas at Austin, is one of them. You can find a link to his remarks in the Resource section. Do this! It is well worth it. You can thank me later.

This speech has since been turned into a best-selling book by the same name. And I can tell you that, since hearing this former Navy Seal's address, I have made my bed every day, at home, on vacation and during business trips far and wide. Admiral McRaven's message is that it is possible to change the world by committing to do the small things, like making your bed every day, with a real commitment, real discipline.

If it is possible to encourage people to believe something can be solved, they are moved to take action. Giving them a reason to believe that a problem – *their* problem – can be resolved inspires action.

PR is often enlisted to help change behavior or create a 'call to action.' The action could be anything from seeking information, visiting a website, downloading a coupon, participating in a contest, liking a social post, sharing a video, talking to a doctor or other professional, beginning a new dialogue or changing the dialogue, following a healthier lifestyle, buying a product or considering a different point of view. Or, any number of other actionable steps.

'Motivation' has become kind of a throwaway word to me. Many PR briefs – the background, goals and objectives documents that clients provide to PR counsel they're retaining for a new project – ask for a strategy and activations that motivate stakeholders in some way or another. That has certainly been the case in healthcare, the space I've primarily worked in for more than 30 years. Likewise, many talks I've heard at sales meetings include a 'motivational' speaker.

The thing is, in my experience, motivation doesn't actually motivate. Something else does.

Some suggest that fear and guilt change behavior. Consider the notion of reminding those who need to check on and improve their heart health that they must do so if they want to be fit enough (read: *alive*) to walk down the aisle at their daughter's wedding or play with their grandchildren. There's a pretty unsubtle 'or else' warning at play there. Maybe this is effective, based on the sheer number of ads, PR programs and quotations in press releases that take this approach.

"

Your beliefs become your thoughts,
Your thoughts become your words,
Your words become your actions,
Your actions become your habits,
Your habits become your values,
Your values become your destiny.

"

My preference, and often my recommendation, is to *go positive* instead. Here is a formula that can be considered for those PR challenges that ask for a call to action or a behavior change:

Offer an image of success. Then add reason and a simple roadmap to encourage trial that leads to habit.

Here are some steps to consider:

1. When your goal is to create a behavior, thought change or a call to action, begin your process with a deep understanding of your stakeholders. Do the research so you understand their emotional triggers, day-to-day lives and challenges.

2. Find your own empathy. Remember that you – the real you, not the 'PR person' you – have something in common with the people you need to communicate with. Bring your humanity to the table.

3. Find the higher truth in your message; this makes people want to take the action you're asking of them. This is more human, less commercial and certainly less promotional. This truth – what we sometimes refer to as the 'higher calling' – is at the top of the message pyramid, and what your stakeholders will find most relatable and most attractive.

4. Often, successful 'asks' or calls-to-action address a discontent or a frustration that is current and on the minds of your stakeholders. As with all the suggestions in this book, this is an idea, not a steadfast rule. Your ask needs to be dictated by your research and the challenge at hand.

5. Whatever the ask is, make it achievable and keep the language you use simple. There shouldn't be any ambiguity. After all, how easy is it to remember to make your bed every day?

6. The ask should be positive and make people who take the action feel good about themselves in some way: physically, emotionally, culturally, spiritually, professionally, as contributing to society or their community.

7. Consider who does the asking. The source of the ask is extremely important. Who is the spokesperson, the source of the voice of your campaign? Are they credible and trusted? Most decisions to change behavior or take an action do not require extensive research – people make decisions like this based on trust.

8. Create a sense of community where people can make their action personal and share their experiences. You can aim to spark a movement or crusade.

Ideally, the action will become a habit, which will, eventually, turn into a value. And then, your PR effort will be a success.

EXERCISE 11

We've all made efforts to break an old habit or form a new one. As discussed earlier, we often do this in January, through New Year's Resolutions. Now, write down three actions you took in the past that were successful in helping you change a certain behavior, and three that weren't. Why did some succeed while others failed?

"

Everything comes to him who hustles while he waits.

"

Thomas Edison

CHAPTER 11
TECHNOLOGY REVOLUTION

In PR, standing still is not an option. Learning and adapting and changing practices and habits are absolute musts. As part of that, staying abreast of new technology and tools is crucially important. Indeed, arguably the most significant 'influencer' of 2024 and beyond is AI. Key to our success is not only how to understand and leverage this technology's benefits but also how to mitigate its downsides and limitations.

Being an early adopter of AI will help you avoid getting left behind.

What should communicators know to prepare themselves to support brands keen to 'flex the muscle' of AI? To answer this question and more, I spoke to Tejas Totade, Chief Technology Officer at Ruder Finn. Here are Tejas' top tips for managing the pace of new technologies:

EMBRACE THE VALUE FOR THE EVERYDAY
New tools can help communicators boost efficiency and productivity. They can take on the 'grunt work.' For example, AI technology can turn a written document into a PowerPoint presentation. It can record a meeting or an interview and immediately provide a summary. AI can also help unlock creativity – it can be used to develop avatars and even virtual influencers, often within just an hour or two. If applied correctly, AI can help get many day-to-day tasks out of the gate pretty quickly.

EXPERIMENT

Take every course or other education and training opportunity available, and integrate what you learn into your day-to-day work. But don't stop there. Carve out an hour or so of your own time to keep learning. For example, research the technologies used by other companies, including your competitors. Even if you don't understand everything at first, this will help familiarize you with the concepts and jargon. A good starting point would be podcasts at the intersection of business and technology. Here are two: Hard Fork from *The New York Times* and *Vergecast*, hosted by Nilay Patel. See the links in Resources.

LEARN WHEN, AND WHEN NOT, TO TRUST TECHNOLOGY

While various AI tools can make getting from point A to point B a lot easier, the information they spit out often includes 'hallucinations,' inaccuracies and misinformation that are presented as fact. For instance, in using AI to compile useful tourism information, output that was published in Microsoft Start's travel pages on places to visit in the Canadian capital suggested the Ottawa Food Bank (which serves the homeless and others in need) as "a tourist hotspot," encouraging readers to visit on "an empty stomach."

These tools will get 'smarter' over time, but for now it's still necessary to take AI-generated content with a grain of salt. Do your own initial research so you begin with good baseline information.

There is no shortage of stories online about the dangers of the spread of misinformation due to AI. Consider this headline in *The Washington Post*: "The rise of AI fake news is creating a 'misinformation superspreader.'" And, there is the case of a New York lawyer who was sanctioned for citing completely fictitious court cases, which were suggested by ChatGPT, in a legal brief.

My last words here: Be careful. Always fact-check the output.

OPPORTUNITIES RIGHT NOW

As the field evolves, there are many ways to gain valuable assistance from AI immediately. For example, communications professionals can use the technology to generate media lists and data sets to reveal patterns and trends, identify influencers, track positive and negative sentiment in online conversations and media, and more. Additionally, the predictive analytics AI provides can help communicators uncover valuable insights for strategy development. Just remember that the more specific the information you provide in the ask, the better the information in the output.

To be sure, new technologies and the resulting tools are game-changing, and there is a sense of relentless momentum in their adoption and utilization in our work. Nonetheless, emotional intelligence, critical thinking and complex problem-solving are innately human attributes. Even the smartest machines cannot inspire or lead. As communications embraces new technologies, it will be up to us to leverage the benefits while maintaining our long-standing commitments to authenticity, trust and relationships. And plain old common sense.

EVOLVING USES OF AI IN PR

Every day we in communications are embracing new ways to leverage AI. For example, this technology has transformed some of our basics such as:

- Media monitoring
- Social listening
- Micro-targeting messaging
- Data analysis
- Identifying gaps
- Flagging brand issues early, if well programmed
- Helping with writing first drafts or wordsmithing a particularly thorny sentence

AI's ability to collect and show information isn't new to most or maybe even all of you reading here. It's only the tip of the value these tools offer for efficiency. The opportunity is how we use the time we get back to lean further into how we bring what makes us and our communications human – intuition, empathy and bold thinking – to the fore

Use of AI in communications – indeed, in most industries – is a hot topic. As with most new technologies, there are good, if not great, game-changing uses. But also areas of caution. Staying current, open and teachable will be the best practice.

"

It's not personal, Sonny. It's strictly business.

"

Michael Corleone

CHAPTER 12
THE HARD WORK OF BUILDING A GOOD CORPORATE REPUTATION

"It's strictly business." What a line. It's one of the most enduring and oft-quoted from Francis Ford Coppola's iconic movie, *The Godfather*. And while I've never found it to be an absolute in every aspect of above-board business (compared to the Corleone family business, which was decidedly more than olive oil), it is a good reminder that the relationships and reputations we're building through effective and creative communications are in the service of business objectives.

A strong, trustworthy reputation is all-important to businesses, in every industry and sector. While it can take years to build a positive reputation, it can take an hour – or even a few minutes – to lose it. A corporate reputation can be negatively impacted, if not seriously damaged, with one viral video or a couple of damning posts from people with significant platforms. The fallout can go straight to the bottom line in a flash.

Consider the share price plummet of United Airlines after a passenger was forcefully dragged out of his seat to make room for a commuting crew member. The incident occurred on April 9, 2017. Two days later, *Forbes* ran a story with the headline, "How United Became the World's Most Hated Airline in One Day." Within a month, a Harris Poll reported that negative perceptions of United's corporate reputation had increased 500%, with 42% of US consumers saying the airline had a 'bad' or 'very bad' reputation. Managing the backlash took months, with United eventually settling a lawsuit with the aggrieved passenger for an undisclosed sum.

Building a good corporate reputation is hard. Sustaining one is even harder. It takes discipline, financial and human resources, time and effort. The good news is that when reputation is a priority at a company, it shows.

While considering how to approach reputation-building, it can be productive to take a step back, and critically assess your company's stated commitment and how it is presented and carried out. You may want to ask yourself and your team the following questions:

- Do our commitments contribute to our reputation?

- Are our company commitments authentically aligned with our values?

- Are we presenting our commitments realistically?

- Are we doing enough to bring these commitments to life for internal and external stakeholders? Do our employees know about our commitments? Are they part of them? Do they live them?

- What can and should we be doing to back up our spoken commitments, with actions that can deliver immediate, tangible benefits to stakeholders? These might include fostering better understanding, distilling new insights that can be acted upon, or making financial contributions that will have a significant impact.

Since the 2017 United situation, there have been (too) many stand-out examples of 'fallen angels' – coroprate or brand reputations that went south in an alarmingly short time (e.g. Bud Light, Zara). Fortunately, there are also examples of companies with positive reputations (e.g. Microsoft) as well as those with reputations that had a misstep and subsequently rebuilt (e.g. Balenciaga).

What is perennially clear is that a strong and trusted reputation is a holy grail. Keep in mind two key parts: conveying what the company stands for and making a difference that is positively experienced by stakeholders. When these are in harmony, guided by a coherent message and supported by actions that make a real impact, you're on the right path.

EXERCISE 12: DIFFERENT WORLDS

This exercise encourages you to draw inspiration from unrelated fields or industries, to solve a specific problem or challenge.

Return to the hypothetical fitness app you're tasked with promoting. Now, think about four brands in unrelated spaces (fashion, food, cars, etc.) from which you can draw inspiration or ideas.

Brainstorm how principles or solutions from those fields could be adapted to support your fitness app.

List these observations and how they can be applied.

Reflect on how they could be developed further for the fitness app.

REPUTATION STARTS WITHIN

Many companies say their most important assets go home from the office every night. Reputation work must include communications that engage and inspire, and make employees feel respected, understood and valued.

Internal comms requires careful planning for an overarching strategy, as well as the tactics that bring the strategy to life, frequency, content and style of executive team interaction with employees. And remember, letters, emails and speeches from the chief executive and others in the C-Suite to employees often find their way into the media, deliberately or otherwise.

There are many excellent examples of internal communications that show a clear link to business objectives. The eyeglass company, Warby Parker, made a big splash with its approach to internal comms and employee practices, which had a direct impact on its corporate reputation.

Communiques to employees from Microsoft CEO Satya Nadella are well worth reading. One example that stands out is his email to employees on his first day on the job. "Like you," he wrote, "I had a choice about where to come to work. I came here because I believed Microsoft was the best company in the world. I saw then how clearly we empower people to do magical things with our creations and ultimately make the world a better place." How inspiring.

EXERCISE 13

Read a news article about a corporate reputation – a mishap or success.

Examples:
1. Bud Light and influencer Dylan Mulvaney (2023)
2. EasyJet and broken seats (2019)
3. Positive reputation of Patagonia

Summarize your takeaways.

CHAPTER 13
THE MEDIA

The media are a key stakeholder for any company or brand, and a primary target audience for PR practitioners. As discussed earlier, while many marketing services pay for coverage, PR is the only one that delivers *earned* media. Therefore, cultivating reporters in the space you're working in is critical. Journalists are valued partners with whom you want a strong and trusting relationship.

TEN MEDIA RELATIONS TIPS:

1. Identify the reporters who are important influencers in your space.

2. Keep up with their stories and interests.

3. Follow them on their own social media.

4. Reach out to let them know you liked a particular article or broadcast piece of theirs, and why. It is important not to see your relationship with reporters as transactional. Rather, take opportunities to share an opinion or compliment without having an ask attached.

5. Crisp writing and brevity matters. Your emails should be short and tight.

6. Always proof your written communications – no typos!

7. Respect their deadlines.

8. When you're pitching a story, make it clear why your suggestion (an interview with a company subject expert or opinion leader, a product demo, a facilities tour) is of value to them and their audience.

9. Learn from your experience. Why did the reporter accept some story ideas and not others?

10. Aim to be a valued resource for your target reporters so they reach out to you (and your client) when they need a quotation or can otherwise reference you in a story.

In today's light-speed media environment, being ahead of the curve is not just a bonus; it is an absolute requirement. Because the media is so fragmented, we need to know what reporters are interested and covering. We also need to dissect each outlet not only by section, but also by individual column to find your way in.

"Newsjacking" is another strategy. What I mean by this is spotting a trend or a competitor brand's news, launch or storyline and then working to make your story part of theirs. This requires you to be very aware of what's going on in your space in real time so that you're ready to move in promptly.

It was only a few years ago that the national media was considered top-tier and the most important to get into. It's all different now. Now, with so many destinations for stakeholders to receive the information of most interest to them, in many cases, 'top-tier' media could be a blog or podcast of a newsletter on, say, Substack.

"

Don't let the perfect be the enemy of the good.

"

Voltaire

CHAPTER 14
PERFECTION IS OVERRATED

In a 2017 interview with the *Harvard Business Review*, actor Alan Alda was asked about his reputation as a perfectionist. "I don't think I'm a perfectionist," he replied. "My early training as an improviser got me used to the idea of uncertainty and the value of the imperfect. Everything is a stepping stone to something else, whether it's perfect or lousy. I'm always looking to get better. It will never be perfect."

Everyone who has ever worked in PR – no, make that every human being who has ever worked with other humans – has a war story about a situation that involved memorable imperfections.

Here's one of mine:

I had an ongoing assignment with a long-time pharmaceutical company client. We were responsible for creating the theme and building the educational program for an annual three-day symposium of executives from the managed care industry and the company's own extended team responsible for this area. This was an effective and much anticipated program for relationship building and creating an environment of learning, for both the company sponsor and its stakeholders. My group needed to conduct extensive research to identify the hot topics that kept the audience up at night, and then recruit four or five speakers who could address the various issues involved.

One speaker we pursued was very much in demand that year. He had just been published in an influential journal, was extremely knowledgeable on the most burning issue facing our audience and was quite well regarded. After persistence, a persuasive pitch and some luck, he agreed to be our keynote speaker. My agency team and our client were elated. When a colleague and I finally met him in person during the event's meet-and-greet that first afternoon, he was everything we'd hoped: bright, articulate, happy to be there and chatty with our clients and symposium participants. The PR team was high-fiving each other for our great get.

Then, that evening, at the reception before the meeting was to start the next day, we noticed our guy drinking more than seemed appropriate. He was soon sloppy drunk, and before we knew it, he was relieving himself at the edge of the lawn! We quickly hustled him out of sight, got him back to his room and crossed all our fingers and toes that he'd sleep it off and be bright-eyed in time for his talk 12 hours later. The next morning, our keynote speaker didn't turn up for the sound check or breakfast. He didn't answer his phone. Finally, five minutes before the scheduled start time, he responded to my colleague's frantic knocking on his door. He splashed some water on his face, put on a tie and appeared at the podium to deliver what turned out to be a cogent, thoughtful (though a bit wobbly at times) presentation that drew rave reviews. That year's event received the highest ratings of any the client had ever sponsored.

Was this project a success? It certainly seemed so. Did it achieve its objectives? Yes, without question. But was it perfect? I think we all know the answer to that.

Perfection is not a reasonable measure for most professionals or assignments. PR is no exception here. There are many other more meaningful standards that practitioners can hold themselves to.

On the next page, I have provided ten questions to ask oneself in the development of, and then throughout, any PR assignment or campaign. For me, these are worth striving for, rather than chasing perfection, and truly define the success and value of our industry.

1. <u>IS MY PR STRATEGY ALIGNED WITH BUSINESS OBJECTIVES?</u> How will what I am proposing or doing contribute to the reputation or perception of the company, organization or brand?

2. <u>ARE MY RECOMMENDATIONS WELL INFORMED?</u> Have I considered the day-to-day lives of my stakeholders? Their points of view? Who or what influences them? Do I know, based on this understanding, where we can find agreement between our company's goals or aspirations and theirs?

3. <u>CAN I SUPPORT MY RECOMMENDATIONS WITH EVIDENCE?</u> Have I done my research, with demonstrable data and credible sources? (I don't know about you, but I do not consider Wikipedia an eminently citable source.)

4. <u>HAVE I DELIVERED MISTAKE-FREE DOCUMENTS?</u> Spell-check will not find every mistake. Never could. Never will. Your written output – proposals, presentations, reports, content, press releases, tweets, captions, letters – needs to be carefully proofread. Preferably by humans, and at least two of them. Do not underestimate the value of 'a fresh set of eyes.'

5. <u>HAVE I USED THE RIGHT CHANNELS FOR MY TARGET AUDIENCE'S NEEDS?</u> The range of delivery vehicle options is extensive. The tools we use to amplify our messages can be a game-changer to any strategy. Resist the urge to tap the channels you personally find interesting or useful, and instead consider those that are most consumed and trusted by your stakeholders.

6. <u>DO MY MESSAGES COMMUNICATE WITH INTEGRITY?</u> Remember, we are not spinning here. There is no situation in which you do not want your message to be 100% trusted.

7. <u>DO MY PR RECOMMENDATIONS INTEGRATE WELL WITH THE OTHER ELEMENTS OF THE COMMUNICATIONS MIX?</u> This is especially important in integrated, multichannel efforts and campaigns where PR is at the table with colleagues from Public Affairs, Analyst Relations, HR, Legal/Regulatory, Advertising, Marketing or consulting firms. This is only a partial list of potential partners. PR practitioners can and do collaborate with many other disciplines.

8. <u>HAVE I FACILITATED A TWO-WAY DIALOGUE AND/OR CREATED ENGAGEMENT?</u> Have I inspired? Inserted something new, or changed the conversation about an issue or a brand? Have I made engaging with my brand, company or organization easy to do?

9. <u>AND, IF WE CREATE ENGAGEMENT, ARE WE LISTENING?</u> Then, are we acknowledging and including the differing points of view?

10. <u>FINALLY, HAVE I HELPED TO CREATE AND/OR ENHANCE A RELATIONSHIP WITH MY STAKEHOLDERS?</u> Have I identified areas in which we agree?

"

A day without learning is a day wasted.

"

Albert Einstein

CHAPTER 15
YOUR JOURNEY
TO SMART PR

Public relations practitioners will continue to be the voice of reason, the dot connector, the explainer of why and how companies and their leaders make certain choices, introduce new ideas, brands and solutions, and act in support of stated commitments. PR is also considered the conscience of a company. Communications and the trust that stakeholders have in these words and deeds are central to this.

Every day, there are exciting and inspirational examples of PR-led solutions and campaigns. As you've seen throughout this book, smart PR takes research, thinking, learning, listening and observation. It also takes a fair amount of courage. PR practitioners need to be willing to stand up in a room full of people who need to find a solution and say, if they really believe this is true, that the only real solution is the hardest one. That the quick, simple fix just won't do. Curiosity and empathy are other character traits that PR counselors and practitioners need. Along the way, I cannot overstate the importance of integrity, without which there is no credibility. By integrity I'm talking about real intellectual honesty.

Oftentimes, going back to the roots is the best way to go forward. PR specialists will benefit from the pioneering work and thinking that make our profession valuable, business-critical and a must-have.

This focus on the art of it seems an imperative now, at a time when the buzz around new tools, exciting channels and new media is so dominant.

I also wanted to encourage students of philosophy, psychology, human behavior and other social sciences to feel they have a path into PR. And, conversely, I'd urge journalism, PR and media students to expose themselves to a wider range of classes, such as business and business management. The industry needs all of these skills in order to thrive and continue providing perspective and distinct worth.

There are many resources available that go far deeper on the subjects I've touched upon in this book. I have listed a few of these in the Resources section. The opportunities to read more, hear more, learn more and experience more to improve your abilities as a PR practitioner are practically limitless. I hope you remain curious and read more. Many sage and seasoned professionals who gave so much of their time in interviews with me have written articles and books, rich in experience, vision and direction. They also speak at industry events. I encourage you to seek them out. Be open to learning in all forms. It's possible to gain new knowledge and perspective every day.

Learning is fun. Really. I know this sounds cliché and old school, but get past this. Adding perspectives, seeing things from new angles and being able to express not only your own point of view, but how others feel, builds empathy and understanding – attributes much needed for every public relations professional in a rapidly changing world.

RESOURCES AND FURTHER READING

NOTES TO CHAPTER 2: HOW PR BEGAN

Bernays, Edward L.
http://www.nytimes.com/books/98/08/16/specials/bernays-obit.html?mcubz=3
Further reading: '*Biography of an Idea: Memoirs of Public Relations Counsel Edward L. Bernays* (1965) and *The Later Years: Public Relations Insights 1956-1986*' (H & M Publishers, 1986), edited by Paul Swift.

Finn, David, Ruder Finn
http://www.prnewsonline.com/2012-pr-news-hall-of-fame-david-finn/

The Museum of Public Relations
http://www.prmuseum.org/

NOTES TO CHAPTER 3: CORE TENETS

PRWeek: https://www.prweek.com/us

PRWeek UK: https://www.prweek.com/uk

PRovoke: https://www.provokemedia.com

The Arthur Page Society: http://www.awpagesociety.com

The Institute for Public Relations: http://www.instituteforpr.org/

O'Dwyer's: https://www.odwyerpr.com

Ragan: https://www.ragan.com

Reputation Today: https://reputationtoday.in (I write the 'Shifting Sands' column)

Cannes Liones PR awards: https://www.canneslions.com/awards/lions/pr

NOTES TO CHAPTER 4: PR FUNDAMENTALS

Popova, Maria. 'Chuck Close on Creativity, Work Ethic, and Problem-solving vs. Problem-creativity.' *Brainpickings* (2012). https://www.brainpickings.org/2012/12/27/chuck-close-on-creativity/

Shpigel, Ben. 'With Rigor and Mystique, Nebraska Builds a Bowling Dynasty.' *The New York Times* (2017). https://www.nytimes.com/2017/04/11/sports/nebrasks-bowling-lady-cornhusters.html

Deloitte Consulting LLP. 'Transitioning to the Future of Work and the Workplace.' https://www2.deloitte.com/content/dam/Deloitte/global/Documents/Human Capital/gx-hc-us-cons-transitioning-to-the-future-of-work-and-the-workplace.pdf

Sandifer, Carly. 'Anton Chekhov's Six Writing Principles.' *OneWildWord.com* (2011). https://onewildword.com/2011/11/14/anton-chekhov%E2%80%99s-six-writing-principles

NOTES TO CHAPTER 5: THINK ATTRACTION, NOT PROMOTION

Dyer, Wayne W. 'Success Secrets.' http://www.drwaynedyer.com/blog/success-secrets/

NOTES TO CHAPTER 6: THINK MEANINGFUL, NOT JUST 'SNACKABLE,' CONTENT (FIRST PUBLISHED IN COMMPRO, NOV 2023)

Thomson, David. Are Attention Spans Getting Shorter? The Facts About Focus. https://www.sciencetimes.com/articles/46092/20230920/are-attention-spans-getting-shorter-the-facts-about-focus.htm

Sma, Shalena et al. The Illusion of Multitasking and Its Positive Effect on Performance. https://journals.sagepub.com/doi/abs/10.1177/0956797618801013

Barney, J. B. et al. Create Stories That Change Your Companys Culture. https://hbr.org/2023/09/create-stories-that-change-your-companys-culture

NOTES TO CHAPTER 7: CREATIVITY

Einstein, Albert. n.d. https://www.brainyquote.com/quotes/quotes/a/alberteins121643.html

Liesse, Julie. 'What Clients Want. OMD 10th Anniversary: That Was Then, This is Now.' (2012):c6 http://brandedcontent.adage.com/pdf/OMD10_anniversary.pdf

Lewis, Richard, W. *Absolut Book: The Absolut Vodka Advertising Story.* https://www.amazon.com/Absolut-Book-Vodka-Advertising-Story/dp/1885203292

https://www.unilever.com/news/news-search/2024/20-years-on-dove-and-the-future-of-real-beauty/

2017 Commencement Address at Harvard University, given by Mark Zuckerberg https://www.youtube.com/watch?v=BmYv8XGI-YU

Kelly, Tom. Build Your Creative Confidence: 30 Circles Exercise. https://www.ideo.com/journal/build-your-creative-confidence-30-circles-exercise

CHAPTER 8: LISTENING

Covey, Stephen R. n.d. https://www.goodreads.com/quotes/298301-most-people-do-not-listen-with-the-intent-to-understand

Encounter Communication Guidelines. http://www.encounterprograms.org/wp-content/uploads/2012/07/FINAL-Introduction-to-Ebcounters-Comm-Agreement.May15.12.pdf

Alan Alda in conversation with Neil deGrasse Tyson, 'What Does It Mean to Be a True Communicator?' https://www.facebook.com/92ndStreetY/videos/10154988234193884/?fref=mentions

Seppälä, Emma and Stevenson, Jennifer. (2017). 'In a Difficult Conversation, Listen More Than You Talk.' *Harvard Business Review* https://hbr.org/2017/02/in-a-difficult-conversation-listen-more-than-you-talk

CHAPTER 9: WORDS ARE OUR CURRENCY

Sartre, Jean-Paul. n.d., https://www.goodreads.com/quotes/6300-words-areloaded-pistols

Eminem interview with Anderson Cooper on *60 Minutes*, October 10, 2010. https://www.youtube.com/watch?v=4hrOQ-x-QNM and https://www.youtube.com/watch?v=_kQBVneC30o.

Scrabble®, https://scrabble.hasbro.com/en-us

Bananagrams®, http://www.bananagrams.com

CHAPTER 10: CALL TO ACTION

Angelou, Maya. n.d., https://www.goodreads.com/quotes/5934-i-velearned-that-people-will-forget-what-you-said-people.

McRaven, William H. 2014. Commencement address at the University of Texas at Austin on May 17, 2014. https://www.youtube.com/watch?v=pxBQLFLei70

McRaven, William H. 2017. *'Make Your Bed: Little Things That Can Change Your Life ... and Maybe the World.'* New York, NY: Grand Central Publishing. http://www.mcravenbook.com/

Gandhi, Mahatma
http://www.quotationspage.com/quote/36464.html

CHAPTER 11: TECHNOLOGY REVOLUTION

Hard Fork (https://www.nytimes.com/column/hard-fork,
Pivot (https://podcasts.voxmedia.com/show/pivot)

Vergecast, hosted by Nilay Patel (https://www.theverge.com/the-vergecast)

Verma, Pranshu. The Rise of Fake AI is Creating a Misinformation Superspreader. https://www.washingtonpost.com/technology/2023/12/17/ai-fake-news-misinformation/

Merkin, Sara. New York Lawyers Sanctioned for Using Fake ChatGPT Cases in Legal Brief. https://www.reuters.com/legal/new-york-lawyers-sanctioned-using-fake-chatgpt-cases-legal-brief-2023-06-22/

CHAPTER 12: THE HARD WORK OF BUILDING A GOOD CORPORATE REPUTATION

The Godfather, film, Dir. Francis Ford Coppola, 1972. VHS.
Paramount Home Video, 1999: movieclips.com.
https://www.youtube.com/watch?v=OqvpcfYFHcw

Temin, Davia. 'How United Became the World's Most Hated Airline in One Day.' https://www.forbes.com/sites/daviatemin/2017/04/11/how-united-became-the-worlds-most-hated-airline-in-one-day/#10b721ac61f2

Harris Poll, United Airlines
http://www.theharrispoll.com/business/United-Airlines-Reputation-Nose-Dive.html

Satya Nadella. CEO of Microsoft Email to Employees on His First Day on the Job. https://news.microsoft.com/2014/02/04/satya-nadella-email-to-employees-on-first-day-as-ceo/

CHAPTER 14: PERFECTION IS OVERRATED

Voltaire n.d. https://www.goodreads.com/quotes/search?utf8=%E2%9C%93&q=Voltaire%2C+perfect&commit=Search

Beard, Alison. (2017). Life's Work: An interview with Alan Alda, *Harvard Business Review*. https://hbr.org/2017/07/alan-alda

READING

In addition to staying current on world news, marketplace reporting, industry coverage and pop culture, I recommend the following outlets as part of your regular rotation:

- *PRWeek*: http://www.prweek.com/us
- *AdAge*: Particularly the CMO Strategy: http://adage.com/section/cmo-strategy-columns/481
- *Harvard Business Review*, both the magazine and the blog
- Carol Kinsey Goman, Ph.D. is an international keynote speaker and author of *The Silent Language of Leaders: How Body Language Can Help – or Hurt How You Lead* and *The Truth About Lies in the Workplace*.
- *AP Style Guide* or *The Chicago Guide*
- Encounter Program and Resilient listening http://www.encounterprograms.org/wp-content/uploads/2012/07/FINAL.-Introduction-to-Encounters-Comm-Agreement.May15.12.pdf
- McRaven, Admiral William H. *Make Your Bed* https://www.amazon.com/Make-Your-Bed-Little-Things/dp/1455570249
- Bill Gates message to 2017 graduates https://mic.com/articles/176935/bill-gates-has-a-message-for-every-college-grad-who-wants-to-change-the-world#.84Qc1htod
- Bill Gates commencement message to 2017 graduates: https://www.gatesnotes.com/About-Bill-Gates/Dear-Class-of-2017
- About T. Boone Pickens: http://www.boonepickens.com/
- Susan Fowler, *Motivating People Doesn't Work and What Does: The New Science of Leading, Energizing and Engaging*
- Stephen Covey, *The 7 Habits of Highly Effective People: Powerful Lessons in Personal Change*

For PR history, consider these:

Bernays, Edward L., *Biography of an Idea: Memoirs of Public Relations Counsel Edward L. Bernays*. New York. Simon and Schuster, 1965

Bernays, Edward L. (Swift, Paul, ed). *The Later Years: Public Relations Insights 1956-1986*. Rhinebeck, NY: H&M Publishers

Watching

- Eminem interview
  https://www.youtube.com/watch?v=4hrOQ-x-QNM

- Eminem on '60 Minutes' with Anderson Cooper and rhymes with orange
  https://www.youtube.com/watch?v=_kQBVneC30o

- 2017 Commencement Address at Harvard given by Mark Zuckerberg
  https://www.youtube.com/watch?v=BmYv8XGI-YU

- 2005 Steve Jobs Commencement Address at Stanford
  https://www.youtube.com/watch?v=D1R-jKKp3NA

- 2014 Commencement Address at the University of Texas at Austin
  given by Admiral William H. McRaven
  https://www.youtube.com/watch?v=pxBQLFLei70

Awards

PR case studies of successful campaigns are typically detailed in industry awards programs. There are many very worthy ones. I have provided only a short list below.

- Silver Anvil: http://apps.prsa.org/awards/silveranvil/#.WXDQx9Pyv-Y
- SABRE awards: https://www.provokemedia.com/events-awards/sabre-awards
- *PRWeek*: http://www.prweek.com/us/awards
- Cannes Lions PR Awards: https://www.canneslions.com/awards/the-lions/pr
- *Bulldog Reporter* awards: https://www.bulldogreporter.com/awards/
- The ONE Club: http://www.oneclub.org/

Failures

I also recommend searching for and learning about the PR efforts that were unsuccessful, because these are also hugely instructive. Not surprisingly, these are not archived in any one, neat place. Scour the internet. Talk to people; any seasoned PR executive will have a hair-raising story to tell.

ACKNOWLEDGMENTS

I'd like to thank all the accomplished leaders in our industry I respect and whose work I have followed since beginning my career.

I would not be in PR without the innumerable reporters, editors and writers whose work I have read and admired, and those I am lucky enough to know personally, whose fluency and ability to paint pictures in my head and evoke my emotions leaves me in awe.

My gratitude extends every day to the clients, peers and colleagues I've partnered with over many years. Many of these relationships have grown to valued and enduring friendships. I have learned something from each and every one of them, and benefitted from each and every experience.

Special thanks to Jack Jacob, who persuaded Lewis Wilks, his colleague at the Lansons | Team Farner agency, to generously share his creative playbook of exercises, many of which have been adapted here.

My fellow teachers and course heads in universities at which I've worked or guest-lectured, from New York to Bristol and Mumbai, as well as students in my classes, workshops and boot camp sessions, have been a great source of inspiration to me. The Roman philosopher Seneca said, "While we teach, we learn." This has been true for me. It gives me great satisfaction and pleasure to know the next generation of the PR industry is in very good hands.

Not a day goes by when I don't wish my parents, Rae and Irwin Stahl, who instilled in me the values and perspective that have governed every step I've ever taken, were still around.

To LID! Thank you to Martin, Aiyana, Caroline, Teya and the entire LID Business Media crew for the encouragement, expertise and support for the second time around.

I couldn't accomplish much of anything without the support of Jeremy Jacob, my husband and partner in life, parenting and business, whose love and unfailing, bottomless and selfless support has bolstered me for what seems like forever.

And finally, my love and thanks to my children Sophie, Jesse and Jack, who challenge me every day to think more deeply, read more, choose my words more carefully, have more patience, try harder, exercise more, eat healthier and strive to be an all-around better version of myself today than I was the day before.

ABOUT THE AUTHOR

SANDRA STAHL is co-founder of jacobstahl, a Ruder Finn company since 2020.

Over a 30+ year career, Sandra has worked on both the agency and corporate sides of communications, including launching, building and then selling jacobstahl, an agency she created with partner Jeremy Jacob.

She is recognized for bringing evidence-based, creative counsel and solutions to clients, primarily from the healthcare space, about internal and external communications, executive communications, issues management and corporate responsibility strategy. Particular sweet spots are building and rebuilding reputation and supporting brands throughout their lifecycles.

Sandra is a frequent contributor to industry and national publications and is an award-winning author of three books: *The Art & Craft of PR*, *Shifting Sands: Building Reputation in an Evolving Landscape* and *The Smart PR Book*.

Sandra holds a B.A. in Political Science and Sociology from Queens College, City University of New York. She is founding faculty in the Branding + Integrated Communications master's degree program at CCNY and a frequent lecturer at universities around the world. Mentoring the next generation of communications leaders is a personal passion.

A native New Yorker, Sandra is married with three children.